Quit Your Job
And
Earn Money
From Home

I0485983

By

Michael
Kaltenbrunner

The information provided herein is stated to be truthful and consistent, in that any liability, in terms of inattention or otherwise, by any usage or abuse of any policies, processes, or directions contained within is the solitary and utter responsibility of the recipient reader. Under no circumstances will any legal responsibility or blame be held against the publisher for any reparation, damages, or monetary loss due to the information herein, either directly or indirectly.

The information herein is offered for informational purposes solely, and is universal as so. The presentation of the information is without contract or any type of guarantee assurance.

The trademarks that are used are without any consent, and the publication of the trademark is without permission or backing by the trademark owner. All trademarks and brands within this book are for clarifying purposes only and are the owned by the owners themselves, not affiliated with this document.

Table of Contents

5

INTRODUCTION

With the state of the job market, and wages seemingly stagnating, there are a lot of people looking for new ways to make a living. Even if you already have a job, it's wise to find an alternative way to bring in some money. Diversifying your income streams is a clever strategy. It helps ensure that you will not be left in the lurch, should something go wrong with your main career.

Some people are looking to escape the rate race, and stop working for a boss that doesn't appreciate them. Others would like to increase their standing in life, by raising their annual income. Whatever your reasons, it *is* possible to make money from home.

There are going to people who tell you that it's impossible — they don't have a clue.

Others will agree that there is money to be made from home, but all the good sources of income have been taken by the big boys — they just don't know what they're doing.

Using the information in this book, you *can* finally quit your job and earn money from home. It *doesn't* take years of study or training, or any investment capital. The best part is — you can get started today.

You Don't Need a Degree or Fancy Resume

One of the biggest hurdles supposedly stopping people from making money at home, is that they don't have a university degree, or their resume isn't good enough. Do you want to be successful, and stop working to help your boss's dreams come true? You might have already given working at home a try, and failed to find success. What can you do now?

There's a good chance that you do need more education or training, but those things can come from plenty of sources.

There is a ridiculous number of websites, books, DVDs, cheap courses, and workshop seminars on offer — all the time. Many of them are brilliant and helpful, others are so-so, but then you will also find plenty of garbage. Even the worse ones will usually outline the basics of what you need to become successful working from home.

Of course, lots of people just buy a book, DVD, or sign up for a course, and that's about as far as they get. It's a great feeling to know that you've actually *done* something positive toward reaching your work goals. Of course, no amount of information can force you to be persistent.

Instead of wishing that you had gone to university, or that you just had a little more to put on your resume — why don't you learn the skills, and make the work for yourself?

You Don't Need Skills to Start a Business

It is common for people to think that you need some grand talent, just to start working from home. You might hear others complain and say things like, "I wish I could start working for myself from home, but I just don't have the skills yet." This is especially true for creative things, like art or photography.

Here are two popular myths about the matter:

1. You have to be the best at whatever you want to do.

There are plenty of people who make more money than you would care to think about, when they really aren't that great at what they do. Sure, their customers or clients must be happy with their services, but they certainly are not the best in the business.

2. You need to have the appropriate skills to have a business.

To be a freelancer or employee, using your specific skills for clients or a boss, you do need the right skills. But you don't need them if you want to start your own business. How many rich restaurant owners actually know how to cook? There are many who have never made a meal, but they still earn loads of money through cooking.

You *do* need to be able to organize someone with the necessary skills. After that, you will need people who are willing to pay for those skills. Suddenly, you have your own business, where you make money by organizing jobs to be done.

Stop thinking that you need to wait until you suddenly become the best in the world, or you have all the right skills. Go out and start a home business, if that's what you really want to do.

RETHINK HOW YOU THINK ABOUT WORK

People are often looking for someone to just hand them a "job". It's a common problem in the work from home world.

These are the types of things they say:

"How can I get a job selling things from home?"

"No one is hiring people to work at home. You can't make money that way."

"I wish I could work from home too, but ..."

Surely, if you can't find a job that lets you work from home, there must be no money available, right? Wrong!

When you think about jobs and the workforce, what exactly comes to mind? Many people imagine going for an interview in an office, and trying to convince some arbitrary PR person to give them a job. If they want you, then you can start to work for them until they no longer need you. Otherwise, you head home with your shoulders slumped, and a sour look on your face.

It is well into the 21st century at this point, and definitely time to forget ideas of work that remain from 20 years ago.

To those who would like a regular, dreary "job" handed to them: maybe you should stick to working in an office or factory. For everyone else — people who are willing to find work and make the money come to them in a world of technology — please proceed with this book.

THE TRUTH ABOUT MOST WORK FROM HOME GUIDES

You've probably already seen the advertisements around, telling people they can make loads of cash overnight, without doing any actual work.

"Learn how I made $2,000 in just one day!"

"Earn $80 an hour with no skills, from home."

And the list of variations could go on just

about forever. If you were to actually click on these ads, as you might have, the information that you saw was probably pretty convincing. These "gurus" and "experts" probably presented a lot of "proof" that they make loads of cash every day. Heck, some of them might even make that much money. After all, there are plenty of people out there doing it. The problem is, that their "special" books and products, which will cost you loads of cash, probably aren't all that helpful.

In fact, you might have already known a lot of the information that they contained. That's why you are better off with something more sensible; a book or guide that doesn't promise to make you rich, in exchange for hundreds of dollars. You can learn how to quit your job and earn money from home, but it's not going to be an overnight thing. It will take time and effort, over a period of time — but you will make it!

That's what this book is about: sensible, practical information that you can start to implement today.

STEPS TO CREATE AN ONLINE BUSINESS FOR ALMOST NOTHING

You can't just sign up to some special club, and expect to become rich in a day. There certainly is no "magic" formula for becoming wealthy, otherwise there would be a lot more people living on their own private islands. However, there are lots of great ways to start making a livable income online. All you need to do is stop waiting around, hoping and dreaming —

and put your grand plans into action today.

This chapter will demonstrate how you can quickly set up one of the business ideas listed in this book, for less than $200. In fact, if you really have no cash to spare — you can do it for practically nothing.

DECIDE WHAT TO SELL

Since you want to get started immediately, and you don't want to spend too much money, the quicker dollars are your target. Read through all of the possible home working jobs in this book, and choose a few that appeal to you the most. Now, go through your list and write down the pros and cons of each, as well as any costs that might come with them.

You will most likely want to create a website for your business, which will cost you less than $100, with a domain name and web hosting. You can easily create a site yourself, even if you don't have any experience. That's all covered in this book, so don't worry.

GETTING PAID WITH PAYPAL

You are going to need a way to let people pay you, and PayPal is the top way to do so. Visit their website and register for free, then set up your methods for receiving payments.

MARKET YOUR BUSINESS

You are going to need to draw people to your business, which will require Internet marketing. You can use Facebook or Google AdWords for paid advertising, and their prices are very reasonable. These are the cheapest and most effective methods, without knowing a whole lot about online marketing.

The rest is up to you!

HOW TO MARKET FOR FREE

There are a lot of people trying to get big in their chosen industry. The problem is that there are *so* many products and companies saturating the market, that is is pretty hard to compete. At least, that's what it used to be like before the Internet came along. Luckily, there are now many ways that you can market yourself or what you are selling, but they often cost money.

If you want to quit your job and earn money from home, but a marketing budget is one thing that you are lacking —

check out this plan for marketing yourself for free.

1. Create a Podcast

Podcasts are kind of like radio shows, but they can be downloaded and listened to by people at their own leisure. You can talk about the niche of your business, as well as having guests who can answer your listeners' questions. You don't have to live near someone to have them on your podcast, because it's easy to just record a Skype conversation (with your guest's permission, of course). You can do this with your laptop or smartphone, but buying a decent microphone is a good idea.

2. Start a YouTube Channel

It doesn't matter what business idea you choose to go with, from selling seashell necklaces to building web apps — you should make a YouTube channel. Create a short video every week about what you do, but make sure there is something valuable for users. You can include details about your business website, and tell people that they will find a lot more great stuff there. Use the microphone that you got for step one.

3. Make a Facebook Page

This isn't the same as a user profile. Pages are used by businesses, brands, and personalities, to interact with fans and customers. You should write engaging posts about your business, and what you are offering people. Create about 2 to 5 posts per day, but don't overdo it or you will irritate fans. Take photos of any products that you offer, or share news about your services.

This is an ideal platform for you to get very personal, and interact with people who are fans of your business. It's also a great place to post links to any content that you upload to your website, Podcast channel, or YouTube channel.

4. Blog Like Crazy!

Websites can seem pretty impersonal and dull. If you want to interact with users the most, treat your website like it were a blog. You might want to have a section on your site dedicated to your blog, so that you can maintain the rest of the site as it is. Write personal anecdotes that relate to your business, tell people warming stories about family and friends, and make sure that you always bring it back to your product or service in the end.

5. What Now?

These four steps, once they are all going, will work together to create a huge amount of traffic to your website and other platforms. Your YouTube channel will help to boost followers on your Facebook page, while your blogs will drive people to listen to your Podcasts. It's like a big ol' melting pot of free marketing goodness, and all you need to do is take advantage of it.

SET UP YOUR HOME OFFICE

If you are serious about making a full-time income working at home, you are going to need a suitable place to do business. The kitchen table might work just fine at first, but you will eventually need a space that's dedicated to getting things done.

People often make the mistake of assuming that they can just set up their business in the corner of their living room, or in the bedroom. Think about who uses these areas, and how their coming and going might disturb you.

Accomplishing productive work might not be too easy while your kids are playing their latest video game with the sound turned up. You could always tell them to be quiet (possibly), but that's not really fair, is it? Everyone should feel happy and comfortable in your home, even if you are working there.

The best solution is to set up a home office in a dedicated space, away from distractions. If you have a spare room in your home, great. Otherwise, try to use a corner of your home where people don't tend to hang around too much. An attic or garage might be a good place, even if it needs a little fixing up. Some people even turn large closets or wardrobes into quaint little office areas.

A stable desk with enough space for your computer equipment *and* some books or work resources, is best. You don't want to be resting things on your lap while you are performing computer tasks.

You are also going to need some storage, most likely. This will take up some of your space for work, but it will also help you to organize your office supplies and tools. A good shelf, or some drawers, is usually adequate for small home offices.

GREAT BIG LIST OF JOBS THAT YOU CAN DO FROM HOME

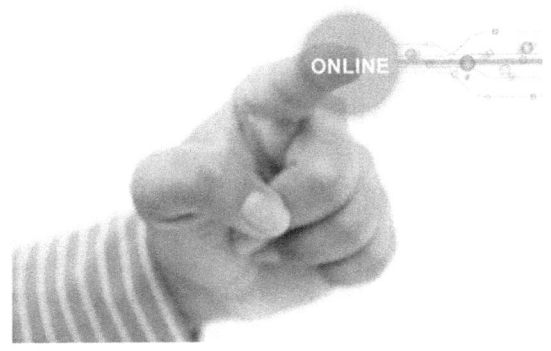

You Can Make Your Own Website

Many of the jobs detailed in this book will work better if you have your own website. It's even a necessity in some cases. Would you like to learn how to make your own site? You probably already know that they are a great way to bring in new clients or customers, and grow your business.

Did you know that a website can even *be* the business, if it's able to attract enough visitors. Of course, you will need to find a good way to monetize all that web traffic (and that's covered after the next section).

Whatever you plan to do with your website, it is a smart idea to obtain a piece of Internet real estate for yourself. There are loads of others making their livings through different online ventures, and many of them rely on a good website to do so. While you might believe that only big businesses or people with

investment capital can have nice websites, that is quite untrue.
It might seem pretty intimidating for someone who's never made one before, but building a website it a fairly easy process these days. Within just a few hours, you can have a complete website, ready to be shown to the world.

WHAT YOU NEED TO BUILD A WEBSITE

Firstly, you are going to need your own domain name, which is the "www" web address. You need to pay a domain registrar to secure one for you. This generally costs around $5 to $15 per year, depending on what you choose, which extras you want with it, and what company you go to. Here are some of the top domain registry companies around:

- Namecheap
- Hover
- Name
- Dreamhost
- Gandi

Secondly, you will need a company to provide web hosting for your site. This is where your website will actually be kept online, so that people can visit it. Here are some popular choices:

- iPage

- Web
- JustHost
- HostGator
- Bluehost

Some of these web hosts have their own site builders, which you can use to quickly get your own site running. If you want the easiest route, you should choose a host that offers this type of tool.

If you don't want to use a basic website builder, you probably have more than basic computer skills. In that case, you can use something like the DreamWeaver creation software, Nvu, KompoZer, or FrontPage. Once you have made your website, you will be ready to upload it to your web hosting.

One of the easiest methods of making a professional site, is to find a web host that provides easy WordPress installation. Most of the good ones do, so you shouldn't have much trouble there. WordPress is a "content management system", that makes it easy to create and maintain professional looking websites.

Once you have a website, read after this

next section, to find out how to monetize it.

MAKE A BLOG

Blogs are basically a form of website, that have their own unique type of formatting and update cycles. They are often about person topics, and can even be used as online journals.

If you think you have something to say, and the world might be interested in reading about it, you can make money with a blog. Since they are typically less formal than books or websites, you don't need to be the best writer in the world. People are often looking for that personal touch, and a sense of personality, from blog writers (known as bloggers).

Start by choosing a topic that interests you, is very popular, or that you feel you could write about a lot. Once you have a nice number of readers, refer to the following section to monetize it.

GET MONEY FROM YOUR WEBSITE OR BLOG

Once you have created a website or blog, you will probably want to know how to make money from it. Keep in mind that you will need to have a lot of valuable traffic hitting your site daily — before you will start to make any real money. This chapter is about telling you how to get money from an already successful site.

These are the top ways to make money off a website:

GOOGLE ADSENSE

This is one of the most popular and lucrative ways to monetize a website. It's not only a good way to make money, but it's relatively easy to use. It doesn't matter what type of website you have, you can display Google AdSense text, block, or banner advertisements. If someone clicks on one of them, the advertiser pays

37

Google, and you get a percentage of that money.
The type of advertising system that Google AdSense utilizes is called CPC (cost per click), because you get paid per click.

CPM ADVERTISEMENTS

CPM (cost per million) advertising platforms pay you every time a page is visiting with an ad. Payments are generally calculated after specific amounts of views.

TEXT LINKS

These can be displayed on any site, and they often look like the content of a page. Just be careful that you don't put them in the way of your content, or users might become annoyed.

AFFILIATE MARKETING

With affiliate marketing, you can make a commission for directing people to certain product sites, but only if they end up buying something. This is a great way to earn money, but you have to have visitors who are willing to make an actual purchase.

SELLING PRODUCTS

Instead of advertising things for other people, and helping them make sales, you can sell products directly from your website.

SELLING SERVICES

Maybe you don't have a product to sell, but rather a service to offer. You might be an accountant who can do people's taxes, or maybe you can paint portraits from people's photographs.

SUBSCRIPTIONS

Once you have a website that provides some serious value to a lot of users, there might be people willing to pay for a subscription.

DONATIONS

Maybe you don't want to sell anything directly. If your users love your site, they will probably be willing to donate to help keep it running. This is a great method to use if you don't want to bother visitors with advertisements.

FLIPPING YOUR WEBSITE

Once your website is getting lots of valuable traffic, and making you a nice monthly income — people will be willing to pay quite well to own it. This is known as "flipping" websites, and you can sell them for up to 20 times a website's monthly earnings.

RENT YOUR WEBSITES

You already know that online real estate can be a great source of income. If you have a successful Internet property, why not make money by renting it out? Just as real estate owners do, you can find people who are willing to pay money to use a webspace that you own. Unlike the physical world, you don't need much startup capital to get started in this industry.

Imagine that you were an expert at making successful websites, and you created a hairdressing site for your local area. You could offer this for rent, to anyone who owns a hair salon in your state. Why would someone be willing to pay money for a website that they can't even own? Imagine how much money some business owners pour into online advertising, even though they don't get more than a few dozen visitors each month.

If your website ranks well with the search engines, and there are hairdressers paying for advertisements in that niche — they would probably love to rent your website. In exchange for their regular rental payments, they would have all of their branding, content, and contact details on your site. It would essentially work as though it were their site, but you would still hold ownership over the virtual real estate.

CREATE A PROXY WEBSITE

Do you ever have trouble accessing websites that you need, when you are using work or college networks? A proxy service will let users bypass those types of restrictions, by going through your proxy website to access their desired content. Some of these services charge customers directly to use their proxies, while others make money through hosting advertisements on their websites. A proxy website can be monetized in a lot of different ways. Just check the laws about them for your area.

CREATE AN ONLINE FORUM

Are you talented at creating social forums in your community, or on the web? Internet forums can make a lot of money, in the same ways that websites or blogs can. The best part is, your users will create new content for you every day, which will allow you to further monetize on your forum.

Post on Forums

If you are a regular member on a bunch of forums, and people seem to like your input, why not use that to make some money? Some businesses will pay people to post on other forums, to create buzz and backlinks for them. There are also freshly built forums that need new users to join in with conversations, to make it seem that there lots of members.

Flip Websites for Profit

You can pretty much think of websites as any other business, or even as real estate. If you are able to create websites that can bring in monthly profits, or even obtain mediocre websites and make them great — you can flip websites for money.

There are lots of investors who are willing to spend money to obtain popular websites and blogs, so they can increase their annual income. If you tap into that market, you can build a site, make it successful, and then sell it to the highest bidder. Sure, you'll miss out on that monthly income, but you can use your lump sum to create more websites.

WRITE ARTICLES

There are a few ways to make money writing articles. Just look online and you will see how common this activity is. If you have a knack for researching and writing about useful stuff, or you have some expert skills to write about, you might be able to make money with articles.

WRITE ARTICLES FOR YOUR OWN SITE

If you choose to create a website or blog, you will need to fill it with content, unless you're selling something. You can either pay writers to do this, or write the content yourself.

BE A FREELANCE ARTICLE WRITER

You can write articles as a freelancer as well. Search online for the most popular freelancing websites where you live, and you can get started immediately.

WRITE FOR USER-GENERATED ARTICLE SITES.

There are popular websites that will pay a percentage of their own advertising income to writers who get a lot of views for their submitted articles.

Here are some popular user-generated content websites:

- Hubpages
- eHow
- Associated Content
- Squidoo
- About
- Examiner
- Google Knol

SELL COPYWRITING SERVICES

If you want to make money writing, but you're not interested in blogging or having your own website, you can sell your services to others. There are more and more people making websites as businesses, but they can't all create the content themselves.

Writing great web copy requires some knowledge of marketing and SEO (search engine optimization). Those are each a whole topic of their own, so this book will not even attempt to cover them in any detail.

To sell your services as a copywriter, go to places like Freelancer or Guru. You can find people who want writing jobs done, and apply for them.

Sell Ebooks

Are you particularly knowledgeable about a topic? Do you think that you could help other people solve problems they have? If you are even moderately capable of writing well, you can write your own ebook and sell it online. All you need is a basic computer with a word processor.

Some nice, free word processors that you can use to create an ebook include Open Office, Abi Word, Jarte, and Neo Office (for Mac users).

After you have written your book, you can save it as a PDF file, and even pay someone to create a book cover for you. Next, you can use networks like Commission Junction or ClickBank to boost your sales, by offering affiliate commissions, or put it up for sale as an Amazon Kindle ebook.

Write Your Own Stories

With great services like Amazon's Kindle,

and Lulu, just about anyone can be a self-published author. If you think that you have a great book in you, why not put in down on the page, and share your story with the world?

You can write short stories, serialized stories, novels, poetry collections, and other works of fiction. Do you have an amazing tale that you'd like to share with the world? Why not turn it into a profitable business, and sell your own stories?

MAKE A WEB COMIC

Do you have a talent for illustration? Why not make a comic strip that others would like to read. You can publish them on your own website, and then use the standard monetization methods of any other site. If your comic gets popular enough, you might try to get it syndicated in popular newspapers, magazines, or websites.

ANSWER QUESTIONS

Do you have a passion for sharing knowledge? You can begin making some cash by answering questions on websites like Ether or JustAnswer. Of course, you won't make much money if people don't like the answers you give, so this isn't the best choice for everyone.

SOCIAL MEDIA PROMOTION

The rise of the social media networks has also made it a necessity for many companies to maintain their own profiles on the popular networks. Unless they are able to completely saturate the market, many multinational companies will not be able to keep their brands above the competition. In order to make their relatively new social accounts seem popular, these companies need to have loads of loyal followers, friends, fans, likes, retweets, etc.

If you have a knack for getting lots of people to follow you on social media sites, why not turn that into a career? You can pay special companies to give your clients more followers or friends. Since many of them offer bulk rates, you can take advantage by purchasing for many clients at once, and even for your own accounts.

If you would rather stay with something a little less unscrupulous, there are plenty of ways to become a professional social media promoter, without buying fans.

SOCIAL MEDIA MARKETING

You probably don't need to be told just how popular social media sites, like Twitter, Facebook, and Instagram are. There are a lot of ways to make money through those sites, but that income generally goes to people who market themselves the best. If you are capable of helping companies with their own social media marketing schemes, you can make some great money.

Some people even get paid to post things to their followers, about certain brands and companies. This can be thought of as a type of sponsorship, really, with people using their own good image to market things for companies. It's not so unusual when you think about it, because offline companies and personalities have been doing the same thing for generations.

SELL STOCK PHOTOGRAPHS

You don't need to be the greatest photographer in the world to start making some money. There are websites out there looking for fresh photos to sell as stock content. Some popular stock photo websites are Fotolia, ShutterStock, Dreamstime, and iStockphoto.

Websites, blogs, newsletters, brochures, presentations, ebooks, and all manner of different mediums need to include pictures. Of course, many people can't afford to pay a photographer to take some special shots. Stock photo companies buy the licenses for them, and then provide access to their customers. Many people might use the same photo for their own products, but it keeps their costs down.

Avoid putting people's faces in your photos, unless you have their legal permission. You should also avoid putting brand names or art works in your pictures, or you might get yourself sued!

WEB DIRECTORIES

If you can create a popular directory of websites, you'll be able charge the owners of websites money to be listed. If you can build your directory up, and ensure that it is respected by search engines and users alike, you can charge quite a nice amount of money to provide backlinks and listings.

TRADE IN DOMAINS

Are you good at spotting when someone has written a link a different way? If you know how to find the Page Rank of a website, or you're willing to learn, you could begin "domaining" for money. This is the practice of trading in domains, where you buy and sell them for profit. You can start for a fairly low investment price, if you don't want to go after the leading domains right away. Many webmasters allow great domains to expire, so you can buy them and then re-sell them for a profit. Try to keep an eye on the sites that are going to be up for auction soon, using websites like Flippa, SnapNames, Sedo, and even eBay.

ARTICLE DIRECTORIES

Many people use article marketing to build their website's presence in the search engines. It all relates to having a lot of links going from other places, to your own site. These are called backlinks. If you create a popular article directory, that the search engines acknowledge as being trustworthy, you can charge money for users wanting to submit their own articles.

Be sure that you only accept articles that are well written and informative. Otherwise, your directory might be black-listed by search engines like Google, and you won't be able to make any money from it.

SOCIAL NEWS SHARING

If you are a well-known user on sites like StumbleUpon and Digg, you can make money to help build up a buzz about products or services. This is not the type of thing that you can just jump into, since you will need to become a power user on these networks first. However, it can eventually be a way to earn loads of cash.

DESIGN OR DEVELOP WEBSITES

There are tons of websites made every day, and plenty of existing ones that are improved upon. These days, it seems that just about everyone needs to have their own website for one reason or another. You can make some money from this trend, by building or designing websites for people, for a profit of course.

You might not know anything about it right now, but you can learn with free online tutorials, or take a course. After a few weeks, you should start to get the hang of making websites. From there, you will need to find people who are willing to pay for your services. Business might be a little slow at first, but once you start to really build your skills up, you will find that this is a very profitable industry.

GRAPHIC DESIGN

Are you great at using Photoshop to create all manner of wonderful design and graphics? You can use those talents to make graphics, stock icons or stock images(similar to how stock photography works), logos, brochures, fliers, or posters.

You can find clients on freelance websites, and then follow their instructions to create something that they can use for their own projects. If you would prefer it, you can sell your work to stock websites, so that you don't have to deal directly with clients.

BE A PROGRAMMER

If you are skilled at computer programming, with any of the popularly used languages, you might be able to make some good money from your home. There are plenty of jobs available on the popular freelancing websites. Register an account, apply for some jobs, and get ready brew some coffee and write some code!

Once you have a reputation for yourself, you should have no trouble finding more work. Previous clients are likely to come back to you for maintenance and upgrades to programs that you made for them in the past, giving you a steady supply of income.

MAKE WEBSITE TEMPLATES AND THEMES

Not every person is able to pay to have a custom website built from scratch. That is a service that costs quite a lot of money, so many people use content management systems, templates, and themes to get the job done. All bloggers or website owners want something that looks professional, and is highly usable. That is why they tend to buy premium website themes and templates, which cost as little as a few dollars, or hundreds of dollars, but look like much more expensive sites.

If you are a designer, you could make your own themes or templates that work with different content management systems, like WordPress or Joomla. One you have some to sell, use a site like ThemeForest to get in touch with buyers. These sites do the rest of the hard work for you, by advertising and processing purchases. They will require a percentage of the sales price in return, however.

Search Engine Marketing

Most of the income streams covered in this book would benefit from some professional search engine marketing techniques. Any website or page that is listed within the first results on the popular search engines, like Google, Bing, and Yahoo, is in a position to make some serious money. Of course, that depends on how valuable the search keywords are that it is ranked for.

Businesses and website owners will pay big money to get their own sites listed first in search engines. If you learn how to do this for them, you could make quite a lot of money, even with just a few clients.

If you would rather not sell your skills to other people, you can just create your own websites. Next, it will be easy for you to make them rank well and bring in loads of valuable traffic.

CREATE APPS

If you are interested in tablet or smartphone apps, maybe you would like to tap into that market. There is an ever-growing demand for more apps, with app builders making loads of money every day. Even if you don't market and sell your own apps, you could learn how to create them for big companies, and earn a living that way.

You don't even need to be skilled at programming to make an app these days. There are many app development services, which are basically apps-for-making-apps. These include AppMakr, iBuildApp, TheAppBuilder, Appery, and Mobile Roadie.

MANAGE WEB APPLICATIONS FOR PEOPLE

Some new webmasters find it difficult to install web applications, like scripts for Joomla or WordPress. If you are able to do the task for them, and people are willing to rely on you, it's possible to make some money doing this. First, you will need to build a name for yourself, as someone who can be trusted with access to other people's accounts.

SELL SOME MERCHANDISE

Have you seen some of the popular t-shirt designs that people wear, and thought, "I could make something so much better." Well, now is the time to put your money where your mouth is, by creating your own merchandise to sell.

If you can make some great designs or illustrations, it's pretty easy and affordable to have them printed on a range of different products. You can get your designs on coffee mugs, t-shirts, greeting cards, posters, key rings and more.

Once you have some merchandise to sell, you can offer them through your own website, or see if an e-commerce store wants to sell them. You just might create the next big merchandise craze, and make a fortune!

BECOME AN EBAY SELLER

There are more and more buyers heading online to make their purchases. The amount of money that goes through sites like eBay has been steadily increasing for some time. If you are constantly finding great bargains on used items, why not buy them, and then make a profit by reselling them on eBay? You don't have to sell used products either, and there are thousands of online stores trading in brand-new items through the website.

ASSIST EBAY TRADERS

If you don't want to start selling yourself, you can assist an eBay trader. Selling hundreds, or thousands, of products every month requires a whole lot of tracking and monitoring. Shipments must be made on time, and everything needs to go smoothly. Otherwise, the seller could find that their rating drops and ruins their income. Many sellers don't want to deal with all of this extra work themselves, or

65

they are just not able to. If you want to get paid to help them, you can register with the eBay Trading Assistant Program.

SELL YOUR OWN CRAFTS

The Internet isn't all about computers and wireless gadgets. Handmade goods, like jewelry, bags, greeting cards, and even key rings, make lots of money too. People are often looking for this type of thing, so why not try selling your own handcrafts on a site like Etsy?

BE A YOUTUBE ENTERTAINER

If you like to be the center of attention, and being on camera does not bother you, why not create your own YouTube channel? Streaming video content is one of the biggest things on the Internet right now, and it has only been growing in popularity.

You can make your own web series, create hilarious song parodies and skits, or make a vlog (video blog) that is seen by millions of people all over the world. There are plenty of people making money with their YouTube videos, and you might be able to become one of them.

It's important that you own the rights to use any brands, music, or images that you place in your videos. Otherwise, you might get in some legal trouble with the copyright owners.

USE AFFILIATE MARKETING ON YOUTUBE

Maybe you're not much of the performing type, but you can still use YouTube to make lots of money. People often prefer to watch a video about something, instead of reading the exact same information in text form. You can use affiliate links on YouTube videos, much like you can with websites.

Even if you don't have any desire to get up in front of a camera, you can still use videos to make money. People often enjoy slideshows that contain nothing but text and images, as well as some royalty-free music in the background.

GAME FOR A LIVING

How many youths have dreamed about this one? While not just anyone can become a professional gamer, due to the level of competition involved in the industry, it is possible. Top ranking players can be paid to play in gaming tournaments, for endorsing businesses and products, or for showing up to gaming conventions and festivals. If you're one of the best at your favorite game, you could start making a living from your skills.

TUTOR ONLINE

Do you have expertise that might help students to get better grades at school or university? If you are capable on tutoring students, you can look for work on one of the popular e-tutoring sites.

Popular sites where you can apply include Kaplan Kids, SmartThinking, InstaEDU, WizIQ, LivePerson, and Sophia.

Your success in applying might depend on the qualifications or experience that you have. In many cases, you will need to pass the test for certification. Once you are all signed up, you can begin helping students with their curriculum, and making money right from your own home as a tutor.

BE SOMEONE'S VIRTUAL ASSISTANT

Small business owners, busy executives, and Internet entrepreneurs often require some help with their daily tasks and administration. However, they might not have enough extra things to do, to warrant hiring someone full time. This is why many people are starting to hire virtual assistants for a relatively small number of hours each week.

You can work online, taking calls or dealing with emails, and have several clients each week. Since many people use virtual assistants when they only need a few hours of work per week, it's a great way to get into online work without making a huge commitment up front.

This is a perfect work at home idea for people who still want to deal directly with people (even though it's all virtual), instead of mostly working alone.

Sell Your Own Web Hosting

This might sound a lot more complex than it actually is. You will not need your own hardware for servers, in order to have your own web hosting business. Many popular web hosts, like GoDaddy and HostGator, allow people to resell their hosting services. Once you have your own reseller account, and you have paid for some hosting, you can charge customers as much money as you like. This is a great way to create a localized hosting service, for people who would rather deal with a company that's located in their home area.

In order to get people to pay extra to buy hosting from you, some sort of unique proposition will be necessary. Maybe you can offer more dedicated technical assistance, or you don't require any sort of subscription.

Perform Microjobs

If you really don't have much time to put into making money online, or you just can't find a useful skill, try taking up microjobs. These are simple jobs that can often be performed in less than a minute. It might be something as basic as liking a Facebook page, or filling out some information in a text field, from a reference text.

While these jobs certainly don't pay much, you can perform many of them at a time. They will quickly add up, and you can get your payment once you reach a certain level of pay.

A popular website for this type of thing is MicroWorkers, but you can also find microjobs on popular freelance sites.

ARBITRAGE SERVICES

If you are good at finding different markets and opportunities online, you might be able to take advantage of the price differences between two different sellers. For example, if you find someone who is buying stock images for $30, you might be able to find another person willing to sell their own for $15. After positioning yourself as the intermediary, you can make $15 per transaction, without needing to tell either party that you were just the middle-guy.

ONLINE RESEARCH

Many writers, students, teachers, and business professionals, need to get reliable information on particular subjects. They don't always have the time, or expertise, to go and find this for themselves. If you are good at tracking down details and data, you could make a living by being an online researcher. Freelance sites are a good place to find clients, as well as other classified services, like Cragslist.

USE GET-PAID-TO SITES

If you don't have any other way to do it, with a skill or business investment, you can still earn money from home. There are lots of perfectly legitimate get-paid-to sites online, where people can make money for reading newsletters, completing surveys, taking part in scientific research, play games, or visiting websites. The pay might not be very high for these tasks, but they don't require any skills, and you can get started immediately.

Just be sure that you don't sign up for a get-paid-to service that isn't going to actually give you your money.

FOREX TRADING

If you think you have a good idea of how currencies change in the market, you can make money as a forex trader. Of course, it will help if you actually understand how the market for currency works, so you might need to take an online course. After that, you can start to trade in forex options, and make quite a lot of money when you get it right.

This is not the type of thing that just anyone should get into. Unlike many of the other jobs in this book, you will need a financial investment up front, and you can lose a lot of money. Make sure that you know what you're doing, if you plan to take on the forex trading market.

MAKE MONEY SELLING DATABASES

This is *not* going to be an illegal tip, so don't worry about that. There are websites that offer sought after data for download. You can access this data, and find a way to compile it in a new and useful way, adding extra value. If you use these lists and then add extra information, which you find from other legal sources, it can be a way to create a high-value product to sell.

SHARE FILES FOR MONEY

Popular (legal) file sharing websites, like Script Mafia, don't just offer their services for free. They make money when people visit their websites, so they need to ensure that there are lots of good files being shared with the public. Many file sharing sites give money to uploaders, each time one of their files gets downloaded. If you can create files that people will want, or you can organize to get the rights to upload them for others, you can use sites like Uploading, Ziddu, and ShareCash.org to make some money.

Conclusion

In the beginning, you might just be making a little on the side. But you can turn that into a full-time gig, and eventually quit your day job *forever*. No one is going to just hand you a nice paycheck for getting out of bed each day. If you think that you can just walk into a cushy job, without any in-demand skills, think again.

Don't get scared, because it's really not hard to break into the world of working online, or just from home. There are plenty of opportunities out there, but you have to be willing to find the niche that best suits you.

Now that you have learned how to quit your job and earn money from home, take a look at this inspiring and poignant quote, which will tell you everything that you need to become successful working from home. If you like, it will be very helpful to write it down and keep it by your work area, to constantly remind you to never give up trying. Good luck!

Nothing in this world can take the place of persistence.

Talent will not; nothing is more common than unsuccessful people with talent.

Genius will not; unrewarded genius is almost a proverb.

Education will not; the world is full of educated derelicts.

Persistence and determination alone are omnipotent.

The slogan 'press on' has solved, and always will solve, the problems of the human race.

-Calvin Coolidge